the verve

POP CULTURE

mad urban soul

Created by Pop Culture, published by Ozone Books, a division of Bobcat Books,
distributed by Book Sales Ltd, Newmarket Road, Bury St. Edmunds, Suffolk. IP33 3YB.
Copyright © 1997 Pop Culture

The author and publisher have made every effort to contact all copyright holders. Any, who for whatever
reason have not been contacted are invited to write to the publishers so that a full acknowledgement may be
made in subsequent editions of this work.

Order No. OZ100045
ISBN 0 7119 6798 9

Picture credits: All Action, Retna Pictures Limited, Redferns, London Features International Limited, Steve
Double, Angela Lubrano.
Cover Picture: Retna Pictures Limited.

Design by: POP CULTURE

the verve

mad urban soul

Velimir Pavle Ilic

introduction

Consider, if you will, the perceived nature of life ooop Narrrrrth. For decades, the area sandwiched between Scotland and the Midlands has consistently been berated and crammed into whippet-rearing, tripe-eating stereotypes, as befits the whim or snide amusement of the non-Northerners who delight in peddling such easy trivia. It is typified by clichéd songs such as 'Life In A Northern Town' by the once-great Dream Academy, led by the equally great but dishevelled Nick Laird-Clowes, an enforced (and perhaps not ideal) ambassador for the region. It has its roots firmly set in bleak 1960s film dramas such as 'A Taste Of Honey' and 'This Sporting Life'. The latter is a particularly gritty portrayal of life in a grim Northern setting, featuring Richard Harris as an uncompromising young coal-miner who tries to better himself by becoming a professional rugby player, whilst becoming involved in a tempestuous affair with his dowdily-attired landlady. Such extreme characterisations may or may not wholly translate into the reality of Northern culture (or any culture, come to that), but the rugby theme is an example where places like the representative town of Wigan have shone over recent years (aficionados will point to a particular chappie called Offiah). Significantly, it is not the only thing that Wigan is renowned for. It just happens to be the birthplace of The Verve, emaciated purveyors of sinuous, acid-flavoured epics and string-tinged balladry, and in truth the unlikeliest candidates ever to even consider gracing a rugby field.

grimly beautiful awakenings

Wigan, 1984, and Richard Ashcroft is 13. Even then, he has decided that he wants to be the singer in a band. He tells his careers teacher so. And even this early on, he is experimenting with the gamut of different haircuts (easy when his mother was a hairdresser). One minute his hair would be bleached blond, the next it would be a dyed-black quiff complemented by sideburns down to his chin. It was easy to find the spark - in 1982, the sudden death, of his father Frank, from a blood clot on the brain, aroused the sensibilities of the young Ashcroft, triggering a reaction in him to do something; the sharp realisation of mortality may have surfaced at the forefront of his mind, but it was never likely to burn negative, wallowing holes in his psyche.

At school he is charmingly regarded as *"the cancer of the class"* (his own words), and is seen as an outsider for whom his teachers have no time. During a Philosophy and Religion exam, Ashcroft decides enough is enough and walks out. It is a gloriously sunny day and if he is honest, he could not give two hoots about the exam. The school became so concerned for his general welfare that, at one stage, they considered dredging the canal in the belief that he had killed himself, unaware that he was sunbathing on a nearby hill, innocently basking in the warmth of the day. Psychiatric help is consequently offered, and befittingly turned down. His outright dismissal of normal nine to five work is confirmed when, under duress, he applies for a job as a lifeguard at Wigan Baths. It is only when he turns up, bereft of a gold proficiency badge, that they realise they have made a mistake, and the indignation of scrubbing the toilets soon follows. Needless to say, they soon see the back of him.

Simon Jones and Peter Salisbury, (who were to become The Verve's bass player and drummer respectively) and Simon Tong (who would link up with the band in 1995) attended the same school, and it was Simon Jones who bore the brunt of Ashcroft's unrelenting enthusiasm. Plagued incessantly by his friend's mouthy desire to become a singer, he recalled in an interview with Exclaim! magazine in 1995 that they *"couldn't play a fucking note"*, and said of Ashcroft's ridiculously lofty ambitions that he has always thought like that. Nevertheless, he had a lot of respect for him.

Peter Salisbury's first meeting with the singer-to-be was also tinged with hostility, the drummer itching to deck him following an argument in the school playground. Tempers soon cooled when it was discovered that all three had a mutual love of football and music. In fact, Ashcroft was a talented footballer - he played for Upholland Boys, and even had a session at Bobby Charlton's Soccer School (the first thing he was told there was that George Best was a prick, a twisted philosophy that was enough to push him away from the sport). During one game, he broke a boy's ankle while both were going for a tackle. It healed sufficiently for Pete Salisbury to take his place on The Verve drum stool some years later.

It was at Winstanley Sixth Form College that the three of them encountered guitarist Nick McCabe, who they had heard playing in the college rehearsal room. His band were scouting for a singer, but once Ashcroft signed up they disintegrated. Jones and Salisbury were quickly recruited, and the quartet decided upon the name Verve (it was not prefixed with 'The' in those days, more of which later). Nights were spent on a hilltop overlooking Skelmersdale, getting plastered on fortified wine and snakebites and ruminating over how rosy the future would turn out to be. Ashcroft's future was given a hearty push at the age of 16 by his stepfather, whom the singer (in an early interview with Cake magazine) described as a Rosicrucian (according to Chambers, *"a member of an alleged secret society whose members make pretensions to knowledge of the secrets of Nature, and transmutation of metals, etc."*). Realising the importance of music and freedom to his stepson, he duly bought him a motor bike, a symbol which gave Ashcroft the scope to find his own feet. The encouragement allowed him to effectively feed his individuality (which was already underpinned by nihilistic tendencies) and gave him a sense of palpable belief. Although never able to replace his natural father, the Verve frontman has always regarded his stepfather as a mentor. He has gone as far as suggesting that his surrogate father is telekinetic, and that by sheer concentration of mind force he can raise the temperature of a room or turn sticks in water! It probably explains much of the spiritual nature of what Richard Ashcroft has to say, and partially explains his exploration of the power of daydreams, visualisation and meditation. From early childhood, he had a well-documented feeling that the whole world was ever-so-slightly unbalanced - the most blatant example ever of the pot and the kettle? - stemming from the day his grandfather showed him the stars at night. It must have been totally bewildering to be told at the age of 5 that space was infinite, and that although the stars could be seen twinkling merrily across the sky, they may not even exist. His resulting philosophy, that the earth is a globe of madness floating through infinity, has stood him in good stead ever since. Eccentric to the last, he was (and still is, to an extent) misunderstood, the subject of much mirth and ridicule in the music media since 1992. Claims of astral projection, and an insistence that humans had the ability to fly, did not help matters; so during the first part of their career, two words became synonymous with any remote mention of Verve (and especially their nutty-as-a-fruitbat singer). For a while he would be known simply as Mad Richard.

Back to the story. After leaving Sixth Form in 1990, life on the dole gave the band the perfect opportunity to sharpen their art. Their first public performance was on August 15th, 1990, at the Honeysuckle Pub in Wigan for their close friend Paul Frodsham's 18th birthday. Incidentally, it was also at this inaugural performance where Wayne Griggs began his career as The Verve's tour DJ; he has played at every one of their gigs since. It was all there. As they jammed, the influence of the past masters, artists permanently etched in the annals of rock history as mavericks and pioneers, could be heard coursing through Verve's narcotic epics, leading some quarters to label them dismissively as sci-fi prog-rockers (Read: Beefheart, Can, Funkadelic, Gram Parsons, Led Zeppelin, Pink Floyd, John Lennon, and Miles Davis for a more definitive analysis). Ashcroft's intelligent appreciation of beatniks like Ginsberg and Kerouac was a vital ingredient to the band's overall flavour, giving their aural tapestry its finishing scent.

Much of the current music doing the rounds had no place in Richard Ashcroft's selective heart (later, once The Verve had become more established, he would view contemporaries (Suede, Blur et al) as formulated combos who lacked any real passion. American music fared no better - he would talk about too much angst-ridden shit coming out of there, and how he felt his own group's compositions were way more messed up than Eddie Vedder's had ever been). At this early juncture however, his dismissal of current British bands did have one high-profile exception, the Stone Roses. Seeing them play in Warrington in 1989, Ashcroft was seduced by their sheer mesmerism, and particularly by the cool allure of singer Ian Brown. He knew then that this was a major indication of his way forward. The Roses were the sublime Mancunian redeemers in the face of so much 1980s bile, and they inspired Ashcroft to assemble what would soon become his own team of Northern champions. Verve were beginning to happen. So fast, in fact, that Salisbury eventually felt confident enough to leave his Ceramics and Geology degree course at Stoke Polytechnic. McCabe left his job as a Trainee Quantity Surveyor in Liverpool, and the band sold rehearsal cassettes to friends in an attempt to subsidise their own gigs in London.

They signed to Hut after their first appearance in the capital in early 1992, a support slot at the Kings Head in Fulham, in front of a paltry gathering barely into double figures. Another supporting show at the London Astoria on February 14th, 1992, (with Smashing Pumpkins and Catherine Wheel) generated a classic early Verve tale. Without the time for a soundcheck, the quartet appeared on stage at the ridiculously early time of 7.30pm, severely narked by how they had been manipulated. Ashcroft began throwing the microphone around, and slamming it into the floor with alarming ferocity. He then proceeded to smash a bottle of water on stage, and for the promoter it was all too much. Just before 8 o'clock he pulled the plug on them, and Verve stormed off stage. As usual, Ashcroft had something definitive to say, using the situation to produce a classy soundbite, *"They might have turned us off, but we've turned you on!"*

chapter two

into the haze

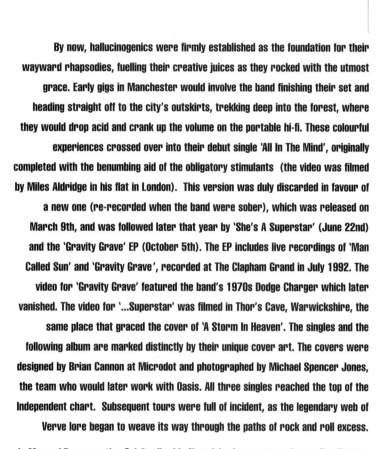

By now, hallucinogenics were firmly established as the foundation for their wayward rhapsodies, fuelling their creative juices as they rocked with the utmost grace. Early gigs in Manchester would involve the band finishing their set and heading straight off to the city's outskirts, trekking deep into the forest, where they would drop acid and crank up the volume on the portable hi-fi. These colourful experiences crossed over into their debut single 'All In The Mind', originally completed with the benumbing aid of the obligatory stimulants (the video was filmed by Miles Aldridge in his flat in London). This version was duly discarded in favour of a new one (re-recorded when the band were sober), which was released on March 9th, and was followed later that year by 'She's A Superstar' (June 22nd) and the 'Gravity Grave' EP (October 5th). The EP includes live recordings of 'Man Called Sun' and 'Gravity Grave', recorded at The Clapham Grand in July 1992. The video for 'Gravity Grave' featured the band's 1970s Dodge Charger which later vanished. The video for '...Superstar' was filmed in Thor's Cave, Warwickshire, the same place that graced the cover of 'A Storm In Heaven'. The singles and the following album are marked distinctly by their unique cover art. The covers were designed by Brian Cannon at Microdot and photographed by Michael Spencer Jones, the team who would later work with Oasis. All three singles reached the top of the Independent chart. Subsequent tours were full of incident, as the legendary web of Verve lore began to weave its way through the paths of rock and roll excess.

In May, while supporting Spiritualized in Norwich, they sauntered casually off stage after only two songs. They reasoned that after driving for six hours to get there, performing in front of fifteen people was not sufficient motivation for a decent set (the rest of the smallish crowd refused to come further forward). It may have seemed selfish, but there was no use in pretending - Verve were not the sort of band to go through the motions. Having a post-gig drink in the bar, they explained their reasoning to the meagre few who had made the effort, and were surprised when they claimed to have understood completely. The apathy continued - an unresponsive audience at London's Town And Country Club goaded them into performing a 25-minute jam of the last song on their set list. If the crowd were not applying themselves, then neither, it would seem, would Verve. Their ability to produce nine-minute singles, coupled with their lambastic stance against what they saw as formulaic music, meant that the world of commercial radio (particularly Radio One) was unlikely to embrace them at this stage.

The imminent summer brought about the next logical step in the book of rock clichés; the band were making their first real foray into the chapter known simply as hotels. After supporting Ride and Spiritualized, Verve set out on their own headlining UK tour on July 8th, 1992. They were staying at the Columbia in London, having invited a group of friends from Wigan to accompany them. Getting the bar manager to stay open all night was a cinch - they offered to buy him a drink every time they bought one for themselves. Needless to say, it was not too long before he had passed out. The hotel master keys were snatched from his slumbering girth, and the Verve entourage proceeded to monopolise the most lavish suites they could find.

October 28th finds the band playing their first gig in the United States, on the back of a flatbed truck in the middle of Times Square. The set is filmed, and includes an extended version of 'Man Called Sun'; later that same day, they play another show at the Tilt club and are given a mightily warm reception. An EP/mini-album is released on December 7th, simply entitled 'The Verve EP'. (Track listing: Gravity Grave (edit) / Man Called Sun / She's A Superstar (edit) / Endless Life / Feel).

March 1st, 1993. A bootleg album is released in America, called 'Voyager 1'. Available only on clear blue vinyl and limited to a thousand copies, it was based on songs that had been recorded live in New York and London during the first few months of 1992. Unfortunately, the release was rendered even more of an instant rarity when 300 copies of it were wrecked en route somewhere between the UK and the U.S. (Track listing: Slide Away / Gravity Grave / One Way To Go / South Pacific / Already There / She's A Superstar). Much of the first half of 1993 was occupied with the recording of their mellifluous debut album 'A Storm In Heaven', which was produced by John Leckie (early Human League, Stone Roses, Cast) at the Sawmills studio in Cornwall. (Track listing: Star Sail / Slide Away / Already There / Beautiful Mind / The Sun, The Sea / Virtual World / Make It Til Monday / Blue / Butterfly / See You In The Next One (Have A Good Time)). Leckie had first set eyes on them at the Falcon in Camden, and was rapidly taken by their soaring, offbeat brilliance; they remain the only combo that he has ever approached with a view to forming a working relationship. The veteran twiddler has frequently recollected the first time Ashcroft tipped up at Sawmills - he had no shoes and no fresh clothing to change into. Furthermore, there was an incident involving both Ashcroft and drummer Salisbury which Leckie also recalls vividly. They had taken a canoe trip down a nearby estuary one evening, with enough draw and bourbon to keep them going for hours. And so it proved.

When they had not returned after a reasonable length of time, the studio staff became worried, especially with it being so dark, and with the approach to the sea only a short distance away. As it turned out, their concern was unnecessary - the pair reappeared a little while later, grinning their heads off and wondering what all the fuss was about. There is also an essence of the Romany traveller hidden in Ashcroft's psychological make-up; ex-manager John Best frequently had the

singer staying at his home, but would discover that his underwear mysteriously kept going missing. Aside from sneaking into underwear drawers, Ashcroft would also mislay or lose his passport with alarming regularity; it got serious when officials suspected him of operating a criminal sideline and selling them on illegally!

A single ('Blue') had been released on May 10th, just after the band had toured with The Black Crowes (incidentally, The Crowes' singer Chris Robinson insisted on performing barefoot on a Persian rug; Ashcroft would later nick the idea). Interestingly, 'Blue' has two videos, one for the UK filmed in Islington, London and another for the USA, filmed in Dublin. Typically, 'A Storm In Heaven' contained none of the singles released thus far (bar 'Blue'), and hit the racks on June 21st, 1993. The album was recorded in Cornwall and contains stunningly ambient brass sections by Kick Horns on the tracks 'Already There' and 'The Sun, The Sea'. The critical plaudits were unanimous in describing it as abstract, illusory, soothing, tinged with feedback, hypnotic, etc. - take your pick. One organ even chronicled it as a gentle psychedelic cacophony, the aural equivalent of sleepwalking. Whatever, it was a league away from Suede, Blur and the emerging Britpop fracas. It may not have been the album that set the commercial globe alight, but it was still good enough to leave the fading baggy and shoegazing scenes trailing in its wake, collectively gasping for breath and unable to focus through the ensuing dust. If you looked hard enough, you could just make out Verve's wiry vocalist in the distance, clicking his heels together before turning into a dot and swaggering over the horizon. With a symbolic nod to the fate of the opposition, 'Slide Away' was released as a single on September 20th, 1993. It wheedled its way across to America, where the song gained valuable airplay and made a significant impact on the influential college charts. 'A Storm In Heaven' also spawned another Verve rarity, a flexidisc of 'Make It 'Til Monday', recorded at Glastonbury 1993. The first steps into the Stateside market had been taken, but events were yet to truly unfold there; events which were to have a profound effect on Verve's plans.

1993 is a busy year for Verve. Their tours include the Lollapalooza in the USA in July and a support slot with the Smashing Pumpkins on the latter's European tour. In September, The Verve play a one off gig at London's LA2 with James, Swervedriver and the Wonder Stuff.

December, 1993. The then little-known Oasis are supporting Verve on their 'A Storm In Heaven' tour. On the Glasgow date, a power-cut leads to Ashcroft, McCabe, Noel Gallagher and Oasis drummer Bonehead (on spoons) performing an *a capella* version of 'She'll Be Coming 'Round The Mountain' and it is at this point that the two bands realise just how much they have in common. It would not be long before Oasis were shaking their laddish banter by the scruff of the neck and shoving it into people's faces, while Verve were content to lay low and wait for their moment. By this time they had already been threatened with court action by the American jazz label of the same name, prompting them to prefix the group moniker. Deutsche Grammophon/Polygram, the multi-national that owns the jazz label, claimed that consumers would become confused, and demanded that the band either pay for extensive market research (to prove that no confusion existed) or pay a fine to the tune of £25,000 and change their name.

So they became '*The*' Verve and prepared themselves for America, particularly the upcoming Lollapalooza jaunt of 1994 (they had considered calling themselves 'Verv', and releasing an album in the US called 'Dropping An E For America' - they decided against it). As preparation for their imminent arrival, a U.S. album release called 'No Come Down', a collection of B-sides and out-takes, comes out, and is intriguing for the live extended version of 'Gravity Grave', which was recorded at Glastonbury in 1993. (Track listing: No Come Down / Blue (USA Mix) / Make It Til Monday (acoustic) / Butterfly (acoustic) / Where The Geese Go / 6 O'clock / One Way To Go / Gravity Grave (Live at Glastonbury, 1993) / Twilight). Although the tour proved successful in a critical sense, it took its toll in another rather serious fashion. The over-indulgent American hospitality and the band's relentless drug abuse had turned them into mental and physical wrecks; events were beginning to turn ominously sour. Ashcroft and McCabe are barely communicating, and at the date in Kansas City, Salisbury (along with one of the roadies) is arrested for causing extensive damage to the hotel furniture. As fate would have it, the combination of the

excessive heat and too much alcohol meant that the very next day, Ashcroft collapsed through dehydration (it later transpired that he was a massive seven pints short of his normal body fluid). According to John Best, it was a case of Richard forgetting to eat food and drink water (as would be sensible in such high temperatures), and he admitted that it was probably the previous night's alcohol binge that did for him. The first signs surface as Ashcroft comes offstage; the venue is not equipped with air conditioning, allowing the searing heat to permeate everything. Complaining of feeling unwell, he is taken to a room backstage and given water, whereupon he begins to shake violently. Their former manager remembers being convinced that he would not make it. Even Ashcroft himself thought his time was up, as he cited in a November 1997 interview with Q magazine's Tom Doyle, *"I was having fits, the whole business. When I was in the ambulance, I remember putting my thumb up, taking the piss. There is a scene in The Simpsons when the stunt rider guy does his jump over the shark pool, puts his thumb up and then he falls in. It was like (laughs), Yeah kids, evil's alright. Funny. But funny and scary 'cause I thought I was gonna die. I had some mad doctor holding me cock while I was trying to pee in a bottle, and two drips coming out of me arms. You just think, Nah, man. I know now I'm really lucky I didn't die."*

The Verve hauled themselves back on stage the following afternoon, with Ashcroft in a state of repressed catharsis. Considering the physical collapse, and his right arm still bearing fresh track marks from the connection to the hospital drip, it was an effort just to stand, let alone sing. It had been a bleak sojourn for the band - the American

american madness

experience had caught up with all of them. The previous day, McCabe and Jones had been perched at the bar of the West Inn Crown Center hotel, and had watched in amazement as their drummer was carted off following his arrest for criminal damage. They had only left him upstairs a short while before. Still, this did not deter them from their drinking binge. In fact, there was a seedy guy at the bar whose wife had just left him, and he was happily plying himself with booze in celebration of the fact. As McCabe and Jones got talking to him, he revealed that he was a phone sex operator-cum-drug dealer, and invited them back to his apartment. One frazzled session of beer and drugs later, Jones had managed to sneak away but McCabe had inadvertently been locked inside the flat and had fallen into a deep sleep. He awoke the next morning, and somehow managed to shuffle his way back to the hotel. The heavy schedule of recording and touring (laced with the now obligatory drink and Class A marathons) had booted The Verve's guitarist into a heavy depression. The tour had turned the four individuals into a shambles. In an interview given shortly after their return, Ashcroft reflected on how the U.S. nightmare had got to him, *"Sticking someone who thinks too much on a chrome bus and sending him around America is not a very good experiment...you wake up in a car park outside some superbowl stadium, twenty-five miles from anywhere, where there's nothing to do but drink. It would get to anyone, that."* Things could only get worse, and they steadily did.

soul destroying

Ashcroft arrived back home in Wigan after the tour to find that his landlord had changed the locks and sold the singer's every last possession (including his father's watch and rings). Hardly surprising when you consider that Ashcroft owed him more than £3,000 in unpaid rent. Then again, he was not renowned for being clever with his capital. The first financial rewards he reaped from the band were spent on... lasagne. For five months, it was delivered daily to his front door, until he eventually ran out of funds. Currently though, his most pressing problem was his lack of abode - he came up with a short-term solution by moving to London, and making a friend's floor his new temporary home. All his remaining possessions were packed in just one bag, but to Ashcroft, this lack of tangible items was strangely intoxicating. Just when he thought that things could not possibly get any worse, the six year relationship with his long-standing girlfriend broke up. The problems had hit a groove, and everything was beginning to show signs of hefty fraying. On May 24th,1994, The Verve were filmed playing a set at Frankfurt Schlathof in Germany, and the curious thing gleaned from this was the two songs they played that had never before been released: 'Black And Blue' and 'Mover'. The former title would be an apt description of how the upcoming turmoil would manifest itself in the months to come.

The recording of the 'A Northern Soul' album did not pass without its headaches either. Taking up the latter part of 1994 and early 1995, it was made under the eye of Oasis producer (and one-time engineer to Johnny Marr's Electronic) Owen Morris at the Loco Studios in rural Wales. (Track listing: A New Decade / This Is Music / On Your Own / So It Goes / A Northern Soul / Brainstorm Interlude / Drive You Home / History / No Knock On My Door / Life's An Ocean / Stormy Clouds / (Reprise)). Many of the sessions were sporadic, ranging from huge jamming sessions that would last three hours or more, to Ashcroft disappearing for five days without informing anyone of his whereabouts.

He would drive around at night for hours, waiting for some flickering of inspiration to hit him between the eyes. Even the studio lawns took a battering - one incident had Ashcroft driving a car round and round in circles, until one of the wheels came off; he continued driving until the grass had become completely cut up. On other occasions, they would all sit around the studio complex and try to get a club vibe going. Generally though, it was an emotionally fraught time for all, with recordings being snatched at all times of the day; the 'History' track was recorded at five o'clock one morning, after Ashcroft played it to the others on his guitar. Drummer Salisbury was duly woken to record his part, and the track was laid down (with strings and Liam Gallagher's handclaps added later at London's legendary Abbey Road studios). It is far and away the best song on the album, with its windswept, bitter sentiment, a gorgeous stringed ballad originally recorded on Ashcroft's home demo tape, using his mother's Spanish guitar, and with lyrics inserted from William Blake's poem 'London'. Blake was the 18th century libertarian renowned for his 'Songs Of Innocence And Experience'; he had inspired the wiry Verve singer because the poem reminded him of time spent wandering around London, getting his head together. Upon hearing the song for the first time, Noel Gallagher was visibly stunned. He did however manage to utter three rather prophetic words: *"Fuck me! Bastards!"*

However, with hindsight, it seems likely that Ashcroft could not exorcise the ghost of his recent break-up with his girlfriend. The ambience in the studios reached fever pitch, as the band strove to attain ultimate perfection and intensity, and relations became increasingly strained. Various factors combined together to breed an uncomfortable working environment - the abundance of ecstasy, endless skinning up, the sylvan quarantine of the location, and the extent to which McCabe had distanced himself from his friends and working companions. Producer Morris was renowned for his piss-taking abilities, and this had undoubtedly affected the sensitive McCabe. There were also some

soul destroying

reports that Ashcroft's forceful personality towered over McCabe's more brittle demeanour - over a period of time, this would also have had a destabilising effect. The guitarist's depression was beginning to envelop him - it had already reverberated amongst the others, and had manifested itself in an aura of understated friction. There was even a stage where Ashcroft, blitzed on virtual hedonism, also began to creep dangerously close to some sort of mental psychosis. Recently, he described how at the time he had ended up in a sleeping bag on the studio floor, with visions of Syd Barrett (ex-Pink Floyd founder, later a diagnosed schizophrenic) flying through his head. It scared the shit out of him - *"..once you lose control over your thought processes to that extent, you're fucked, man. But if you're caning anything, you're gonna get to the point where the demons come, and I was seeing the fucking demons."*

The band were not the only ones affected - events were extreme enough to shove producer Morris (who had alternated furiously between ecstasy and frequent tipples of vodka) hurtling towards the brink of a nervous breakdown. Suddenly, in the flick of a switch, he flipped. Grabbing the nearest chair, he trashed the speaker stack, and then shattered the huge window separating the studio from the mixing room, causing substantial wreckage.

In spite of the torrid circumstances in which it was made, the album was declared a success - a landmark LP flowing with warm, dense and powerful overtones. McCabe's flamboyant electrics were stamped all over it, but sounded especially blissful on 'Brainstorm Interlude' and 'Drive You Home'. It marked a distinct change from the freeform sculpture of their first album, and lyrically the fantasy-based songs had also veered towards the richer realms of Ashcroft's personal experiences. In an interview with Dave Simpson of Melody Maker, Ashcroft all but reveals that his ex-girlfriend ran off with a friend he had known since childhood.

soul destroying

It was patently a sore subject, with the singer's curt responses urging Simpson to move on to another line of questioning. After two or three attempts to glean more information, and with Ashcroft becoming increasingly agitated, Simpson wisely decides not to pursue the matter any further. As for the album, Noel Gallagher declared it the third best record of the year, after Paul Weller's 'Stanley Road' and Oasis' own forthcoming album,'(What's The Story) Morning Glory?'; notably, it would also feature prominently on many end of year review lists (in NME, Melody Maker, Select et al). With the intensity and imagery emanating from it, the success was not surprising, but the nature of these elements could have had dangerous implications - the emergence of obsessive attention, of the ilk given to Richey Edwards or Kurt Cobain, for example. Ashcroft is certainly enigmatic enough to rank with them, but is fortunate enough to have withstood the temptation of the all-important self-destruct button - just. There is still too much to do, and if you are of the belief (as The Verve are) that the mythical power of rock'n'roll transcends fashion and genre, then you should be allowed to express that without being seen as some sort of lunatic. Exhibitionism is being swallowed by the world of commercial music trends - too many bands are playing it safe. Thank God some are not prepared to compromise. The Verve are not an overtly political group, but their songs contain almost subliminal messages, hiding a loathing of upper class rationale; they are not the sort of individuals to be stifled by dogma. As Ashcroft once said, *"...there's a darker side to this country, and I'm its flag-bearer."*

Later that summer, the band played gigs in support of the album, yet although the music press seemed confident in the foursome's unquestionable right to take on the world, The Verve at this point were ominously unhappy with the way their journey was stuttering along. And the curse continued - In April, after an astonishing performance in front of a partisan gathering (supporting Oasis at the Bataclan in Paris), McCabe became involved in a fight with a Parisian bouncer.

Having forgotten his pass, he had tried to gain entry backstage, but for some reason the bouncer took exception to this and threw the unfortunate guitarist against a wall, before punching him in the face for good measure. After examination by a French doctor, it transpired that McCabe had broken one of his fingers, and The Verve were forced to cancel four of their UK tour dates (in Manchester, London, Leicester and another gig supporting Oasis at the Sheffield Arena).

A short time after they returned to English shores, 'This Is Music' appeared as a single on May 1st. 'On Your Own' was subsequently released on the June 5th, with the accompanying video shot by Jake Scott (son of 'Blade Runner' director Ridley). Based in part on Fellini's classic 1974 epic film 'Amarcord' (a fantasy vision of the director's home town during the period of Fascism), it features a host of freakish extras, cavorting through an artificial scene of beautifully photographed lush fog. Both singles entered the Top 40 singles chart that summer. The rescheduled dates take place later that month to affecting reviews in the national music press. Paul Moody, reviewing The Verve's gig at the Manchester Roadhouse, (NME, 17th June, 1995) described them as *"distorted, clean, obscene, beautiful,"* a contradicting perception that was becoming common amongst journalists striving to describe the band's eclectic sound. Richard Ashcroft was also particularly fussy about how the band were appreciated in both media and public circles; there is an example of this which highlights both Ashcroft's eccentricity and his belief that the music should be right. He played a set of new songs to a close friend and asked his opinion on them. Great, replied the friend. Pressing him further, the singer enquired whether the songs were in fact the best he had ever heard. No, said the friend, which gave Ashcroft all the justification he needed to scrap them and begin penning others which were better, more worthy.....the best there had ever been.

The Oasis/Verve double act reconvenes in August 1995, at the Hultsfred Festival in Sweden. Both camps are based at the same hotel, so one night, purely for the hell of it, they decide to embark on a colossal drinking spree. The hotel bar has foolishly been left under the charge of a young, inexperienced female employee; Richard and Noel take advantage of the situation and, fuelled by copious amounts of alcohol, proceed to wreck it. They are ejected forthwith, and go on a prompt search for something else to drink. Finding a church, they break in on the pretext of looking for communion wine. None was found, but the episode was a further indication (if one were needed) of the explicit male bonding and camaraderie that had evolved between the two kindred spirits, even if they did make the front pages of the Swedish national press. It almost goes without saying that the church had to be re-consecrated.

6th August, 1995. Only Richard Ashcroft would know it at the time, but it was to be a fateful day for The Verve and their many disciples. This time, the pulsating chords were to be of no avail. Having just finished what was, by their standards, an average performance at Glasgow's T In The Park Festival, Ashcroft informed John Best that he no longer wished to continue, having cited the fact that it no longer felt right. The band effectively split, but the timing could not have been worse. 'A Northern Soul' had been received extremely well, and having already been lauded with lashings of critical acclaim (in both the UK and the US), the band were about to embark on a path to commercial success. If truth be told, there was no other resolution - talk of an irrevocable rift between Ashcroft and McCabe meant that breathing space was called for, even though three months of tour dates were already lined up world-wide (including more Oasis support slots). Ashcroft makes himself unavailable for any immediate comment, and disappears on a impromptu camping trip in the West Country. Maybe he was in no fit state to make the decision to quit after the

a final history

debilitation of recent months, but it had happened and for the moment that was the end of it. The time spent away from each other would be an immense relief, but that is not to say that the split was not upsetting. Shortly after it had happened, Ashcroft moved to Bath, where he lived for a while writing songs. In several interviews, he recalled the time he spent holed up in a Cornwall hotel after the break-up, in a room that overlooked the cliffs. Radio One was on in the background, and without warning it announced: *"The Verve are history, and this is their final single 'History'..."* Understandably, the singer was choked - more choked than he had ever been in his life, which was logical because Richard Ashcroft was the biggest Verve fan in the world. No-one really doubted that The Verve would return in some form, but at this point it was impossible to make sense of anything.

Salisbury and Jones were the next to drift away, leaving McCabe with no choice but to accept defeat and go back to Wigan. It would be eighteen months before he spoke to any member of The Verve again. He spent time at his mother's home, dabbling in electronica and home-made techno, but the split had ultimately given rise to further depression and mood swings. While his mother was out of the house, he took the opportunity to vent his anger and frustration on the interior decor - crockery and bits of furniture were opportunely thrown about as McCabe struggled to cope with his mental imbalance. Things became critical enough for her to believe that her son was psychotic, and she would constantly plead with him to go and see a doctor. Slowly, he began to come to terms with himself, and what had happened with the band. He even contemplated going back to his old job in Liverpool, but it seemed the most important thing he lacked was a feeling of value from people close to him. His surrogate family may have deserted him, but it had not stopped them from moving on. A single, 'History', was released as planned on the 18th of September, on two separate CDs. Both sleeves depicted the band standing in front of old New York cinemas, but with different slogans emblazoned over the front of each building. Spookily enough, they were rather apt: "ALL FAREWELLS SHOULD BE SUDDEN" and "LIFE IS NOT A REHEARSAL."

a circular reincarnation

Within two weeks of the split, Ashcroft, Salisbury and Jones had recruited old school friend Simon Tong (on guitar and keyboards), and were working together with John Leckie on new material. Rumours abounded that the new band was merely a vehicle from which to expel McCabe legitimately, but although they had adopted a code of silence over the real events leading up to the split, it was unlikely that they were using his severe depression and seclusion as sole reasons to rid themselves of him. Other factors, such as McCabe's preference for the more experimental side of The Verve's music, may have had a part to play in proceedings. When Tong joined, McCabe felt anger and bitterness from afar; he was drowning in a sense of loss, and feeling as though his family and whole world had collapsed. Initially, the new quartet decided not to work under the name of The Verve, but it was not long before they had changed their minds (a point to note here was that all the studio tapes were originally stickered with Ashcroft's name, possibly with a view to releasing solo material). Bootlegs of these supposedly solo tapes were being shifted excitedly from pillar to post, but the singer was not completely satisfied with them, refusing Hut permission to release any of the songs.

November, 1995. In an interview with Select, Noel Gallagher was discussing each individual track on the then new Oasis album '(What's The Story) Morning Glory?'. A track called 'Cast No Shadow' caused particular interest - it was written about and inspired by Ashcroft (no, it does not refer to his stick insect-like build!), painting a portrait of him as a visionary undermined and betrayed by tone-deaf philistines. The Oasis man talks about Ashcroft's perfectionist streak, saying that he never seemed to be happy with what went on around him, and was always seen to be trying too hard to please people by saying the right thing. Inevitably, it would always come out the wrong way. Gallagher was simply reciprocating an earlier gesture - Ashcroft had written the lyrics for the lead track on 'A Northern Soul' after hearing that the guitarist had stormed off Oasis' 1994 American tour, following a much-publicised rift with his brother Liam.

a circular reincarnation

However, the flame flickered within The Verve (albeit gently), and they continued to assimilate rough tracks very quickly (working with John Leckie and Owen Morris, respectively, although neither session was to bear any real fruit). The search for another lead guitarist had begun, but press interest had begun to wane as time ventured into the fallow period of 1996 (during this period of upheaval, the band were paid on a weekly basis by Hut, their record company). In March, Ashcroft received a telephone call from Noel Gallagher, asking if he would be interested in playing a short acoustic set supporting Oasis at Madison Square Gardens, in New York. With nothing to lose, his flight paid for, and all the drink and drugs he could muster on offer, he agrees. So it ensued that Richard Ashcroft made his first live appearance since the split, on Thursday 14th March, 1996. Coming on stage unannounced, he played acoustic versions of three songs: 'The Drugs Don't Work', 'Space and Time' and 'Sonnet'. He went down a storm, but he had not felt comfortable performing without his band - *"I ain't a solo artist. I was put on this earth to be part of The Verve, and make sure I can take it as far as I possibly can. That's my ambition for the next few years."* Further shows were mooted (again supporting Oasis at Knebworth and Loch Lomond), but nothing ever got past the planning stage. It would have impeded the path of The Verve anyway, and that was certainly something Ashcroft wanted to avoid at all costs.

At a party for comedian Eddie Izzard, Ashcroft stumbled across the recently departed Stone Roses guitarist John Squire. The possibility of jamming together cropped up, but a drunken discussion ended in nothing more than idle banter. Squire was doing his own thing and politely turned the offer down. The next suggestion in line was ex-Suede hero Bernard Butler, but this did not hit home with everyone - Jones was keen, Ashcroft remained sceptical. Nevertheless, he agreed to meet up at Butler's house on the pretext that it would be nothing more than an experimental session. It proved to be a success, yet would be short-lived. Ashcroft declared Butler to be perfect, and predicted confidently that The Verve would be the greatest rock 'n' roll band in creation. Typically, it did not work out. They may have had a mutual admiration for each other, but Butler wanted to use The Verve as a showcase for his own songs as well as Ashcroft's. They could never have co-existed under such circumstances, so whilst there was still a shred of dignity to retain, the alliance was broken before it had even begun. It had taken just a week for Ashcroft's euphoric prophecy to fail, but the breakdown of the brief collaboration with Butler was undoubtedly the best possible outcome for all concerned. If the previous situation with McCabe had been perceived as troublesome, then one dreads to think about what sort of havoc a potential Ashcroft/Butler partnership would have wreaked, especially considering the latter's stormy relationships with Brett Anderson in Suede, and subsequently with singer David McAlmont. The clash of egos would have been wholly intolerable...

chapter eight

comebacks and coronets

January, 1997. It was barely a week into the new year. By now, the quartet had collated fifty or so rough demos, but even though the framework sounded good, something was missing. They all knew it. Perhaps Ashcroft realised it more than the others, as he was the one who had instigated the final split. Only he was able to slot in the last elusive piece of the jigsaw. Unhappy with the overall feel of the new material, the band felt the impetus just draining away, and it was going to take something pretty extraordinary to stem the flow. After all, The Verve were a band with their own unique melting pot, a cauldron filled with layer upon layer of tangled, overt emotion. If rekindling it to boiling point was the aim, then the next step was obvious, if far from easy. Ashcroft was quite aware of the remedy. Picking up the telephone and calling Nick McCabe was a decision he had been wrestling with emotionally for quite a while, knowing that in all probability, he would have to eat humble pie. After all, he wanted McCabe back as a musician and a friend, and perhaps more importantly because the guitarist was a person he greatly admired (John Leckie had described him similarly as the real genius behind the music). Ashcroft's sentiment was the vital factor in terms of the positive effect it was likely to have on McCabe's frail confidence - it would probably even go some way to alleviating the lack of trust he had in his former cohorts. Besides, Ashcroft's spiritual advisor - a member of the Spiritualist Church, not far from his London home - recommended that he should re-conscript McCabe to the line-up.

Finally, after much deliberation, Ashcroft succumbed to good sense. He called him up, and asked the guitarist to return to the fold, telling him that if he did not, it would signal the end of the singer's involvement in music. Thankfully, he agreed, claiming later that Ashcroft had been forced to *"eat shit"*. Once upon a time, even that remark would have caused unspeakable tension between the two, but they had come through that. They know how to deal with it. Ashcroft and McCabe may be polar opposites (McCabe once harboured thoughts of causing the vocalist real harm), but they have become protective of one another. It runs through the whole band. With Simon Tong staying on despite McCabe's re-emergence, the bond and the sound has grown. There is even the odd bear hug going around. Far from threatening their kudos, their stature has developed beyond recognition. God knows what they would have done if McCabe had said no...

In much the same vein as Ian McCulloch's, Will Sergeant's and Les Pattinson's feelings on the 1997 re-union of Echo And The Bunnymen, Richard Ashcroft and Nick McCabe could never feel truly complete being part of any other band. As Ashcroft stated in an interview with the NME in June 1997, *"...nothing other than The Verve was gonna do for me."* And so it proved. The music press were delighted to have them back - in March, Melody Maker and the NME both ran stories informing anyone who wanted to listen that the combo had risen from the ashes. You could not really blame them, as they had both championed the band since the very start. A date had already been set for the Reading Festival, and the group were in the studio with producer Youth (former Killing Joke bassist whose previous credits included Polly Harvey, The Orb, U2 and Nick Cave), working on the first part of their forthcoming album. Sessions took place at the Metropolis and Olympic studios in London, although The Verve ended up producing the LP themselves, with help from long-time confidante and engineer Chris Potter. After a sabbatical of eighteen months, the first single to be released from it was on June 16th. 'Bitter Sweet Symphony', a gorgeously crisp abundance of skipping strings atop Ashcroft's emotionally-charged voice, sees The Verve crashing in at No.2 in the U.K. singles chart (selling 300,000 copies along the way, and only beaten to the summit by Puff Daddy!). World-wide, it becomes a huge smash hit. Not surprisingly, it is also NME's Single Of The Week (there was also a James Lavelle remix version issued on July 28th). The video (directed by Walter Stern, who was also responsible for The Prodigy's 'Firestarter' and 'Breathe' promos) sees Ashcroft walking down the busy Hoxton high street, staring straight ahead and knocking people over who dare get in his way. His alert, focused demeanour transmits through the screen and sends tingles shivering down the nation's collective spine. Weeks later, Ashcroft is walking innocently to the local grocery emporium for a pint of milk, when a car screeches to a halt in the street and the driver informs Ashcroft wryly that the video has finished. A case of fantasy merging with reality, but if you are the spindly singer in The Verve with a fondness for living it large, then there is no dividing line. What begins as a simple errand transmogrifies into a full-blown pictorial epic, or at least it does if, like the lanky Ashcroft, you happen to live in South-east London. The Verve had returned in astronomical style, with some purpose, and the public were eager for more. The venues and arenas awaited.

trauma, love, transgression...

Comeback dates were announced in June, with tickets selling out almost immediately. Everything was going so well - until the curse struck again. Ashcroft became ill with a viral infection (singing at rehearsals brought him to virtual collapse), and was ordered to rest for six weeks. The band were reluctantly forced to call off their upcoming tour, and reschedule dates for August. Despite rumours to the contrary, there were no sinister reasons for the cancellation, although Ashcroft was spotted at a Spiritualized gig during his supposed recuperation. He had hooked up with Spiritualized's Kate Radley a while ago, (although at the time of writing, her former band partner and ex-beau Jason Pierce still lives with Radley's parents). Much of their 1997 album 'Ladies And Gentlemen We Are Floating In Space' centres around the heartbreak of the Radley/Pierce separation. There is no doubt about Ashcroft's feelings for his partner - in an interview with Sylvia Patterson of Vox magazine, (October 1997) he claims it is love, threatening to hit out with a baseball bat at anyone who unjustly demeans the couple in print. There is a sign that Ashcroft is becoming niggled by the analytically intrusive side of the press, his tolerance ever-decreasing. He tells Patterson that, *"... I'm not here to be fucking... analysed. I shouldn't have to deal with it. That's the hardest thing to deal with in all of this, without a fucking doubt."*

And the traumas go on. Even the glory of 'Bitter Sweet Symphony' had been tainted; it had come to light that its string and bell loop had been sampled from a version of the Rolling Stones 'The Last Time', on an orchestral LP of Stones hits arranged by Andrew Loog Oldham in the 1960s. Originally, The Verve thought they would have to pay out approximately half of the royalties from the track to Mick Jagger and Keith Richards, who had both expresséd an appreciation of it, but an objection was lodged by the legendary Allen Klein, the Stones' former manager, who owned the publishing copyright on the song. What Klein actually wanted amounted to full publishing royalties from the single, reasoning that he blatantly objected to anyone tampering with the untouchable Stones music. Somewhat ironically, Ashcroft and co. had received a letter from Loog Oldham in which he declared his admiration for 'Bitter Sweet Symphony', and said that the Stones were probably too long in the tooth to remember exactly where they nicked it from in the first place. The song itself is undoubtedly the best single of the year by a mile. Or six. As a nation, we became steeped in its hypnotic tone. While The Verve were playing in Dublin in August, they were informed that the punters in one Dublin bar had adopted it as their anthem, and during the evenings it was hardly ever off the jukebox. A simple night out could easily turn into a comprehensive Verve karaoke, sung with gusto by groups of roaring drunk young men.

trauma, love, transgression...

The band were busy, and were diversifying - Ashcroft had been recording with DJ Shadow for an album of collaborations on the MoWax label (Shadow had labelled rock and dance a good clash), although his participation meant nothing more than going into the studio and laying down a vocal track in four minutes flat. Meanwhile, the rescheduled gigs were doing a brisk trade - touts at London's Hammersmith Palais (August 14th) were asking upwards of £80 per ticket. After only a handful of dates, the voice of The Verve's human beanpole had already started to crack, having been taken to the limit during the passionate shows already completed. It mattered not - the singer survived on surges of adrenaline, as the band simulated an atmosphere at the Palais uncannily akin to the Led Zeppelin gigs of the early 1970s. Ferociously hot it may have been, but flying in the face of it, The Verve pulled off a brilliantly unnerving show. The pandemonium was carried up to Glasgow, where nine hundred ticketless fans attempted to storm the entrance of the famous Barrowlands venue. Inside, The Verve were embellishing their comeback with waves and torrents of beautiful noise. NME's John Mulvey was clearly impressed by it all, talking of a *"fierce magic"* and how his trousers spontaneously split apart during a *"gut-wrenching"* performance of 'History'.

trauma, love, transgression...

There are moments on the rest of the tour that induced small
shivering shocks of emotion, and reduced attentive audiences to mere
gibbering bags of crumpled skin and bone. Like the date at Sheffield's
Leadmill, where they took to the stage to an intro of the Electric
Prunes' 'Holy Are You', and proceeded to plough straight into the
heady notes of 'A New Decade'. Magical indeed, and one of those
snatched, feelgood intros of rock concert history. Some are never
documented, some are forgotten, while others remain lodged in the
sentimental sanctum of the heart. Like the fifteen-minute intro film at
the Manics shows of 1996/97 (projections of radical statements and
images set to the orchestral backing of 'A Design For Life'), these
flashes bring a lump to the throat, and illustrate part of what people
are searching for when they go to such events. There is an
expectation that something electrifying will happen, something that
drives a wedge into the base of your spine, enabling tingly bubbles to
be transported up through your shivering backbone and into your
brain every time you subsequently recall it. The Verve's live sets of
1997 were generally of this revelational ilk; after all, it is a two-way
thing. Both the band and their audience were seeking the same high,
the same cleansing of spirit - the occasion allowed them to haggle
with each other, trading shamelessly in fragile eggshells of emotion.
The band's appearance at the Reading Festival (headlining the Melody
Maker stage on August 24th), also ended in victory, Ashcroft
bounding on while Metallica and Marilyn Manson played the main
stage. The pulsating tent became malleable putty in his hands as The
Verve laid bare their power. Almost unrecognisable as the wigged-out
group of 1993, their tide was finally beginning to turn, with possibly
the biggest transformation in fortune ever witnessed in rock history.

However, as one might expect by now, the single's success was not without its hiccups. A dispute with ITV's The Chart Show meant that they would not broadcast the accompanying video, (which was directed by Andy Baybutt and George Hanson and was filmed at the flat of Hut supremo Dave Boyd, in London). The furore kicked off when the band insisted that it be screened in its entirety, and without the amateurish graphics usually deployed by the Saturday morning music programme. The Chart Show refused, but claimed that Ashcroft was dragging up an old vendetta. A spokesman for The Chart Show explained that he had actually seen the singer at a Spiritualized gig, looking fit and well, when The Verve had just cancelled their U.K. tour due to Ashcroft's supposed illness. He went on to claim that this had got the band into trouble. Manager Jazz Summers criticised the show for their stance, and refused to send them a copy of the tape. The Chart Show did acknowledge the band's position at the Indie chart summit, but were forced to play a snippet from the 'Bitter Sweet Symphony' promo instead (it simply resulted in the Portishead video being given a more extensive showing).

If The Verve thought they had had enough exposure to the full-beam media, and had won the battle with their two singles and tour jubilation, then they were wrong. The acid test (pardon the pun) was still around the corner, with three nights at Earls Court supporting Oasis (25-27 September, 1997), but there was no need to fret. Everything went as well as it could, although taking the stage at 7.30pm meant that the arena was still fairly cold. It soon warmed though as The Verve played a selection of tracks from 'A Northern Soul' and 'Urban Hymns', yet predictably it was 'Bitter Sweet Symphony' that had people rushing in from the bars, spilling their precious, over-priced beer as they just caught a glimpse of Simon Tong beginning the song's sampled string loop on his keyboard. Ashcroft bellows out his customary battle-cry of *"Come On"*, revving up the crowd as he goes. It was generally the same procedure for all three nights, but Steven Wells' perception of The Verve's frontman in his NME review was spot-on - *"Ashcroft pulls open his ribcage, plucks out his battered heart and squeezes it until it spurts dark poetry."*

chapter ten

subliminal peaks

Back in 1993, Richard Ashcroft knew that The Verve were going to be massive. Even then, he was imposing opinions on unsuspecting journalists, and he made one particular statement which turned out to have eerie repercussion - *"I'm into great music; Funkadelic, Can, Sly Stone, Neil Young, jazz. I can name you fifty bands who are doing OK now, and in two years they will be forgotten. History will forget them. But history has a place for us. It may take three albums, but we will be there."* Turns out he was not joking. With the release of 'Urban Hymns' on September 29th, 1997, this promise was fulfilled - and then some. (Track listing: Bitter Sweet Symphony / Sonnet / The Rolling People / The Drugs Don't Work / Catching The Butterfly / Neon Wilderness / Space And Time / Weeping Willow / Lucky Man / One Day / This Time / Velvet Morning / Come On). Garnering vehemently dramatic reviews from the press, the LP had almost made its mark even before it had been released. With the sleeve's design and photography respectively carried out by long-term associates Brian Cannon and Michael Spencer Jones, it had finally made its way into the trembling hands of public and media alike. The Verve family had come full circle across a long, rough sea littered with endless obstacles. Perhaps the curse was subsiding...

With its mid-tempo range and rotund timbre, 'Urban Hymns' comes over with Roxy Music-isms a-plenty. There are countless properties on it that can be attributed in part to classic albums of the past - Pink Floyd's 'Comfortably Numb', Van Morrison's 'Astral Weeks' and The Stones' 'Exile On Main Street', to name but three. Andrew Collins, of Q magazine, interpreted it as having *"cloudbursting skills"*, while B. D. Niven (Uncut, October 1997) got right under its skin to deliver the following salient statement, *"...if dark feelings are big enough, if they're ten times larger and more intense than life, then they're just as attractive, just as inclusive. The album's impelling guitar rhythms again serve to justify Nick McCabe's tortured genius, now the pressure on him and the others has eased somewhat..."* The review goes on to explain how the band have come to accept each other's personal demons. They now work together to understand them, rather than regard them with garish scrutiny.

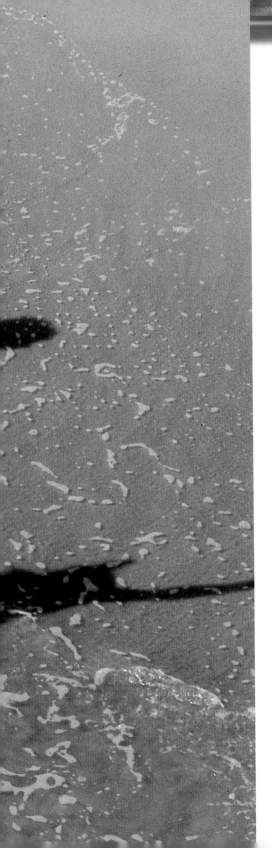

NME's Ted Kessler endorsed the impact of the all-new Verve outlook in his succinct appraisal of the album, *"...the first five songs here pound all other guitar albums this year (bar Radiohead's 'OK Computer') into the ground with their emotional ferocity and deftness of melodic touch"*. To an extent that is true, but there is an incorporeal ethos behind the LP that can be difficult to fathom, as on 'The Rolling People', a nod to The Stones 'Gimme Shelter', which starts with ennui-laden desperation and winds up bathing in supernal positivity. The lyrics have always focused on existence, life-truths and a whole host of disparate philosophies, but the underlying theme has always been Richard Ashcroft, as he himself admits, *"...one minute I'm Dolly down the market selling kippers and the next I'm Lucy In The Sky With Diamonds. I'm the same soul put in a different context."*

The Verve have come quite a distance. Why, they even enjoy daytime Radio One coverage, along with previously discarded peers like Spiritualized and Radiohead. There is even a Scottish novelist called Alan Warner who uses the band as a reference point in his works of fiction. As if to illustrate this further, Ashcroft's many emotionally-pervading guises are summed up for the sake of one rounded purpose - to send out a message and convert people, but still to be what they want him to be.

The Verve have always subconsciously courted bad luck. No-one else could have mishaps on such a grand scale - take Glastonbury 1994: Pete Salisbury broke his ankle as he slipped on the kitchen floor, going for a glass of water. He consequently had two metal plates and six pins inserted into his foot, and needless to say the festival trip was off. They actually managed to get there in 1995, but Nick McCabe's amp blew just as the live TV feed was about to pick them up.

subliminal peaks

What has changed is the way Ashcroft is perceived. His bizarre on-stage behaviour and trademark stare into the audience may have helped to earn him the Mad Richard tag, but it is noticeable that no-one is using it anymore. People are referring to him again as Richard Ashcroft. - a sign of the band being taken seriously? Perhaps. What is more crucial, is the level footing they have sustained recently with Oasis. Perceptions change; once, it was Oasis versus Blur, but having become Oasis versus The Verve, it is an entirely different narrative. There is no hate-filled rivalry, no bitching, no venomous, ill-wishing war of words. Both agendas portray a willingness for success, and if their hallowed paths happen to meet...well, all the better. After a few beers, they will slap each other on the back until the next time. And there are sure to be plenty of those, for it is as the good shaman Jim Morrison once preached, *"there are no limits, no laws..."*, and they have surely paid homage to that over the last few years. Ashcroft embodies Morrison's twisted romanticism, his unearthly passion for the mind-altering experiences of the other side; like Morrison, you get the sense of a Baudelaire, or a Rimbaud, but where the latter's fascination with gun-running may have constituted escape from modern civilisation, Ashcroft's bravado is more in tune with downing a couple of pints of Guinness with his morning coffee. In between cigarettes, of course.

October, 1997. The Verve announce tour dates for January 1998 in Glasgow, Manchester and London, and are planning more extravaganzas at disused airstrips and dry docks later in the year (subject to permission from the Ministry of Defence). Predictions are rife that they will soon overtake Oasis, whose 'Be Here Now' album was, if truth be told, a lazy sideways step that did not win them any new friends, and probably alienated a few of the existing ones. The resurgence of The Verve is partly to blame for that, but Noel Gallagher's continual endorsement of them during their enforced absence helped levitate the pedestal in Ashcroft and Co's favour. With the phenomenal success of 'Urban Hymns', the album sold a quarter of a million copies in a week, Richard Ashcroft can afford to smile, as his star soars into the ascendancy. For the first time in his life, he believes in the power of the galaxy, and the 'neon wilderness' he thought was crazy has suddenly started to make a little more sense.

discography

singles

All in the Mind/One Way To Go (7", 4/92)

All in the Mind/Man Called Sun/One Way To Go (12", 4/92)

All in the Mind/One Way To Go/Man Called Sun (CD, 4/92)

She's A Superstar(Edit)/Feel (7", 6/92, No.66)

She's A Superstar/Feel (12", 6/92)

She's A Superstar/Feel (CD, 6/92)

Gravity Grave EP (Gravity Grave [Edit]/Endless Life/She's A Superstar[Live at Clapham Grand 17/7/92]) (10", 10/92)

Gravity Grave EP (Gravity Grave [Extended Version]/Endless Life/A Man Called Sun[Live at Clapham Grand 17/7/92]) (12", 10/92)

Gravity Grave EP (Gravity Grave [Extended Version]/Endless Life/A Man Called Sun[Live at Clapham Grand 17/7/92]/Gravity Grave[Encore][Live at Clapham Grand 17/7/92] (CD, 10/92)

The Verve EP (Gravity Grave [Edit]/A Man Called Sun/She's A Superstar [Edit]/Endless Life/Feel) (Export CD to U.S., 3,000 held back for U.K., 1/93)

Blue/Twilight/Where The Geese Go/No Come Down (10", 5/93, No.69)

Blue/Twilight/Where The Geese Go (12", 5/93)

Blue/Twilight/Where The Geese Go/No Come Down (CD, 5/93)

Slide Away/6 O'Clock (7", pink vinyl, 9/93)

Slide Away/Make it 'Til Monday (Acoustic)/Virtual World(Acoustic)(12", 9/93)

Slide Away/Make it 'Til Monday (Acoustic Version)/Virtual World(Acoustic Version)(CD, 9/93)

This is Music/Let the Damage Begin (7", burgundy vinyl, 5/95, No. 35)

This is Music/Let the Damage Begin/You and Me (12", 5/95)

This is Music/Let the Damage Begin/You and Me (CD, 5/95)

On Your Own/I See The Door (7" green vinyl, 6/95, No. 28)

On Your Own/I See The Door/Little Gem/Dance On Your Bones (CD, 6/95)

On Your Own/I See The Door (cassette, 6/95)

History (Radio Edit)/Back On My Feet Again/On Your Own (Acoustic)/Monkey Magic (Brainstorm Mix) (CD, 9/95, No. 24)

History (Full Version)/Grey Skies/Life's Not A Rehearsal (CD, 9/95)

History (Radio Edit)/Back On My Feet Again (cassette, 6/95)

Bitter Sweet Symphony (Original)/Lord I Guess I'll Never Know/Country Song/Bitter Sweet Symphony (Radio Edit) (CD, stickered digipak, 6/97, No. 2)

Bitter Sweet Symphony (Extended Version)/So Sister/Echo Bass (CD digipak, 6/97)

Bitter Sweet Symphony (Original)/Lord I Guess I'll Never Know/Country Song/Bitter Sweet Symphony (Radio Edit) (cassette, 6/97)

The Drugs Don't Work (Radio Edit)/Three Steps/The Drugs Don't Work (Demo) (CD, digipak, 9/97, No.1)

The Drugs Don't Work (Full Length)/Bitter Sweet Symphony (James Lavelle Remix)/The Crab/Stamped (CD, digipak, 9/97)

The Drugs Don't Work (Radio Edit)/Three Steps/The Drugs Don't Work (Demo) (cassette 9/97)

albums

A Storm In Heaven (LP, gatefold sleeve, 6/93, No. 27)

A Storm In Heaven (CD, 6/93)

Star Sail/SlideAway/Already There/Beautiful Mind/The Sun, The Sea/Virtual World/Make It 'Til Monday/Blue/Butterfly/See You In The Next One (Have A Good Time)

No Come Down (export CD for U.S., 5/94)

No Come Down/Blue(USA Mix)/Make It 'Til Monday(Acoustic)/Butterfly(Acoustic)/Where The Geese Go/Six O'Clock/One Way To Go/Gravity Grave(Live Glastonbury'93)/Twilight

A Northern Soul (2-LP, with inner sleeves, 7/95, No.13)

A Northern Soul (CD, foldout digipak with postcards, 7/95)

A Northern Soul (CD, 7/95)

A New Decade/This is Music/On Your Own/So It Goes/A Northern Soul/Brainstorm Interlude/Drive You Home/History/No Knock On My Door/Life's An Ocean/Stormy Clouds/(Reprise)

Urban Hymns (2-LP, with inners, outer printed mailer, 5,000 only, 9/97, No. 1)

Urban Hymns (2-LP, with inner sleeves, 10/97)

Urban Hymns (CD, 9/97)

Bitter Sweet Symphony/Sonnet/The Rolling People/The Drugs Don't Work/Catching The Butterfly/Neon Wilderness/Space And Time/Weeping Willow/Lucky Man/One Day/This Time/Velvet Morning/Come On